S0-BFE-957

Witness History Series

THE UNITED NATIONS

Stewart Ross

The Bookwright Press
New York · 1990

Titles in this series

The Arab–Israeli Conflict
China since 1945
The Cold War
The Origins of World War I
The Russian Revolution
South Africa since 1948
The Third Reich
The United Nations
The United States since 1945

Cover illustration: UN poster for a meeting in Maiden Lane in London, England.

First published in the
United States in 1990 by
The Bookwright Press
387 Park Avenue South
New York, NY 10016

First published in 1989 by
Wayland (Publishers) Ltd
61 Western Road, Hove
East Sussex BN3 1JD, England

Library of Congress Cataloging-in-Publication Data

Ross, Stewart.
    The United Nations/by Stewart Ross.
        p. cm.–(Witness history)
    First published in 1989 by Wayland Publishers Ltd.,
East Sussex, England.
    Includes index.
    Summary: Examines the founding of the United Nations,
its work in peacekeeping, human rights, and human welfare,
and its methods of functioning.
    ISBN 0–531–18295–9
    1. United Nations– History–Juvenile literature. [1. United
Nations.] I. Title II. Series
JX1977.Z8R63 1990
341.23–dc20   89–9747
                                                        CIP
                                                        AC

Phototypeset by Kalligraphics Ltd, Horley, Surrey
Printed by Sagdos S.p.A., Milan

Contents

1
A FALSE START
World War

MEN AND WOMEN HAVE always dreamed of creating a world of peace. The Old Testament prophet Isaiah foretold of the day when people would

> . . . beat their swords into plowshares and their spears into pruning hooks; nation shall not lift sword against nation, neither shall they learn war any more.[1]

As century succeeded century, however, Isaiah's prophecy seemed no nearer coming true. Wherever man was, it seemed, war was not far away. Several European writers suggested ways in which conflict might be limited, although their interests did not really extend beyond Europe. Dante, the

fourteenth-century Italian poet, suggested a single system of law for all countries. In 1595, the French Duke of Sully advocated a world army to keep the peace; while the Quaker, William Penn, considered that if all people spoke the same language, we would be much less likely to go to war. Nothing came of these ideas.

Then, between 1792 and 1815, Europe witnessed a long and very destructive period of warfare. The statesmen who met at Vienna in 1815 established, in the Concert of Europe, a system of discussions and alliances that enabled the continent to remain at peace for longer than it had ever

A scene from the Battle of Waterloo, 1815, which cost the victors 15,000 casualties – yet more men died in just the first hour of the Battle of the Somme, July 1916.

been. But the accord did not last. In 1914 a European war started, the like of which had never been seen before, which spread over the whole world.

World War I was fought on and under the sea, in the air, and on land. It destroyed four empires. Almost thirty million servicemen were killed or wounded, and about half that number of civilians also died. The war cost hundreds of billions of dollars and touched the lives of people all over the world.

Previous wars had been fierce, cruel and bloody, cities had been devastated and fields burned, but during World War I, the airplane, the torpedo, the machine gun and poison gas ensured that war became total, involving all a nation's population and all its resources. In such a costly conflict there could be no real victors. Never again, thought the peacemakers who gathered at Versailles in 1919, would such a devastating conflict be allowed to happen. The Great War, they believed, was indeed the war to end all wars.

▲ "A French soldier's last salute," 1915. During World War I machine guns, shells and poison gas led to millions of casualties.

▼ Trench warfare, 1915. In the light of such slaughter and destruction, politicians were determined that in the future nations should learn to live in peace.

The League of Nations

In January 1918, while the fighting was still raging in Europe , U.S. President Woodrow Wilson put forward Fourteen Points as a basis for future peace. The last of these points read:

> *A general association of nations must be formed under specific covenants for the purpose of affording mutual guarantees of political independence and territorial integrity to great and small states alike.*[2]

Already, in Britain, France and the United States there were League of Nations societies to promote such an association. Thus, when the slaughter finally stopped late in 1918, politicians of many nations eagerly cooperated in the creation of a League of Nations.

The Covenant of the League was written into all the peace treaties that followed the war. Switzerland offered itself as the host

President Wilson (left) and other officials in 1917, when the United States entered World War I. The president entered the war reluctantly and was anxious to make sure that victory would lead to a lasting peace.

nation. By 1920, forty-two nations had joined, by 1934 the number had risen to fifty-seven. All member countries had a vote in the Assembly that met in Geneva, and a Council of at first eight, and later fifteen, nations met to ensure the maintenance of world peace. At The Hague in Holland an International Court was established to hear disputes between nations. The League was served by a large Secretariat that dealt with its administration.

The League had four aims:
- To maintain world peace.
- To encourage countries to reduce their armaments.
- To improve the conditions of life for all people.
- To ensure that countries' independence and frontiers were secure from aggression.

In several fields the League was successful. Disputes between nations were settled amicably: for example, in 1925 the League stepped in to quell a border flare-up between Greece and Bulgaria, and in the same year it oversaw a series of international treaties at Locarno that guaranteed the frontiers of Germany. In 1928 sixty-five nations signed a pact condemning war as a means of solving international disputes, and a World Disarmament Conference met in Geneva in 1932.

Meanwhile, the League's Agencies and Commissions worked in a number of humanitarian fields. The International Labor Organization tackled problems such as child labor and safety at work. Led by the famous explorer Fridtjof Nansen, the League helped millions of homeless refugees, while other Agencies sought to end slavery, drug abuse and other international scandals.

Yet, within twenty years of its establishment the League had collapsed. The countries involved had failed to find a means of keeping the peace.

Belgians made homeless by the fighting in World War I. One of the most important tasks that faced the newly formed League of Nations was to help the millions of European refugees to find homes and work.

Failure

The Covenant of the League of Nations was written into the Treaty of Versailles, which dictated the terms of Germany's surrender. President Wilson accepted the Versailles Treaty, but it also had to be accepted by the Congress of the United States.

Senator William E. Borah roared his objection to joining the League of Nations and its Council:

> . . . when you shall have committed this Republic to a scheme of world control based upon force, upon the combined military force of the four great nations of the world, you will have soon destroyed the atmosphere of freedom, of confidence in the self-governing capacity of the masses, in which alone a democracy may thrive. We may become one of the four dictators of the world, but we shall no longer be master of our own spirit.[3]

Borah's words carried the day; the Senate refused to ratify the Treaty of Versailles and the United States never joined the League of Nations. The USSR was not invited to join the League. Germany joined in 1926 but left in 1933, after which the USSR decided to come in. The power and prestige of the League was adversely affected by the absence of several great powers.

Another problem the League faced was getting its decisions enforced. In 1923 the Italian dictator Mussolini invaded the Greek island of Corfu. Perhaps the League, set up to keep world peace, should have used armed force against the Italians. The League hesitated, and Mussolini had his way.

The cartoon below was drawn in 1929, ten years after the establishment of the League. It expresses the generally felt disappointment with the League's progress. Its failure to achieve disarmament among nations seemed likely to lead to war.

This cartoon, published in December 1929, shows Peace (on the donkey) complaining, "This looks very like the point we started from."

German troops occupying the Polish capital, Warsaw, in 1939. Unfortunately the League of Nations was unable to stop such aggression.

In 1935, twelve years after the Corfu incident, Mussolini invaded the poorly defended African state of Abyssinia. The Emperor of Abyssinia came before the Assembly of the League and pleaded:

> *I . . . am here today to claim that justice which is due to my people and the assistance promised to it eight months ago . . . I assert that the problem submitted to the Assembly today is a much wider one than . . . a settlement of Italian aggression. It is the very existence of the League of Nations.*[4]

His words were like a prophecy. The League had already failed to stop Japanese aggression into Manchuria in northern China in 1931. Now it could offer Abyssinia only weak economic sanctions against Italy that did not even include oil or steel. By May 1936 Mussolini's armies were in the Abyssinian capital of Addis Ababa. The League had failed.

Some of the Italian troops who were wounded when Mussolini, ignoring the League of Nations' vain protests, seized Abyssinia in 1936.

2
THE UNITED NATIONS
New beginnings

Winston Churchill and Franklin D. Roosevelt meet during World War II. The "Atlantic Charter" produced by these two leaders contained the seeds of the United Nations.

TWO YEARS AFTER the beginning of World War II, the British Prime Minister Winston Churchill met with U.S. President Franklin D. Roosevelt. Between them they issued an Atlantic Charter, setting out their aims. Apart from the defeat of Nazi Germany, they sought peace, freedom, collaboration and security among nations, overseen by "a wider and permanent system of general security." Churchill asked for an "effective international organization," but Roosevelt would not accept this; perhaps he was thinking of 1919.[5] Nevertheless, the Atlantic Charter is generally recognized as containing the seeds of the United Nations.

In January 1942 twenty-six countries signed a Declaration of the United Nations, accepting the principles of the Atlantic Charter. As the war progressed, its cost in terms of human suffering became more apparent, and the need for an organization to replace the failed League became urgent. In 1944 ideas for the International Monetary Fund and International Bank for Reconstruction and Development (the World Bank) were discussed. Later that year representatives from the USSR, China, Britain and the United States met at Dumbarton Oaks in Washington, D.C. to draw up firm proposals. In February 1945 Churchill, Roosevelt and the Soviet leader, Joseph Stalin, accepted further details, and the USSR at last agreed to come into the new organization.

Peace came to Europe in May 1945, but the responsibilities on the shoulders of the victors were heavy, as this contemporary cartoon (left) indicates. The picture shows three nationalities.

Finally, fifty nations at the United Nations Conference on International Organization, meeting in San Francisco between April and June 1945, drew up the United Nations Charter. On October 24, 1945, after this Charter had been ratified by all the major states of the world, the United Nations came into being:

We, the peoples of the United Nations determined to save succeeding generations from the scourge of war, which twice in our lifetime has brought untold sorrow to mankind, and to reaffirm faith in fundamental human rights . . . and to promote social progress . . . and . . . to practice tolerance . . . and to employ international machinery for the promotion of the economic and social advancement of all peoples, have resolved to combine our efforts to accomplish these aims.

Accordingly, our respective governments . . . do hereby establish an international organization to be known as the United Nations.[6]

▲ This cartoon entitled, "And now let's learn to live together," shows soldiers of the three victorious allied armies in 1945.

► Hiroshima, 1945. Over 200,000 people died and countless others were injured when an atom bomb was dropped on the city. The invention of the A bomb encouraged the formation of a United Nations.

A world parliament?

Although it first met in London, the United Nations (or UN) now has its headquarters in New York, in the magnificent glass-sided United Nations building. Here it sets about achieving its three main purposes:

- To maintain international peace.
- To develop friendly relations among nations.
- To cooperate internationally in solving international economic, social, cultural and humanitarian problems and in promoting respect for human rights and fundamental freedoms.[7]

The only time that all member nations actually meet together is in the General Assembly, a picture of which you can see below. Here representatives from each of the 159 states that make up the UN gather to discuss the world's problems, and how to solve them. In a sense, the General Assembly is like a world parliament, although unlike a parliament it has little power to get anything done. A former UN Secretary-General, Kurt Waldheim, described the organization as "a Tower of Babel."[8] By this he meant that each nation is so eager to make its own voice heard that it does not listen to anyone else. There are five official languages at the UN – Chinese, French, Russian, Spanish and English – but simultaneous translations of speeches are made into other languages.

The Assembly meets once a year, although it can be summoned for an emergency session in a crisis. This happened when war broke out in the Middle East in 1967. Much of the Assembly's work goes on in its six committees:

First Committee – major political questions; there is a Special Political Committee that looks at current problems, for example, apartheid.
Second Committee – economic and financial matters.
Third Committee – social, humanitarian and cultural matters.
Fourth Committee – colonial matters.
Fifth Committee – administrative and budgetary matters.
Sixth Committee – legal business.

In spite of all the hours of talking and piles of papers it produces, the General Assembly cannot really do much. It can:

- Debate any topic it wishes.
- Adopt resolutions, with a two-thirds majority, but these are not binding on member states.
- Help elect members of other UN bodies.
- Elect the Secretary-General and vote on the admittance of new member states.
- Vote the UN Budget.

The influence of the Assembly, therefore, "depends on its moral authority."[9] Some feel that this would be increased if very small states were not granted membership, or if votes were weighted in proportion to the size of a country's population, or if speeches were strictly limited in length.

◄The General Assembly of the United Nations. Representatives of the 159 member nations assemble here annually to discuss their common problems.

►The organization of the United Nations. Although it is easy to criticize the UN, it remains a heartening example of how people can work together in peace.

THE UNITED NATIONS SYSTEM

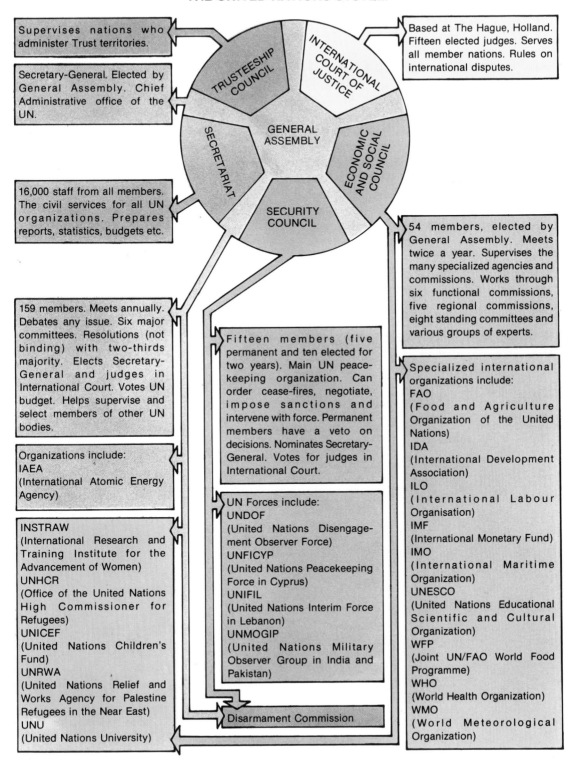

Supervises nations who administer Trust territories.

Secretary-General. Elected by General Assembly. Chief Administrative office of the UN.

Based at The Hague, Holland. Fifteen elected judges. Serves all member nations. Rules on international disputes.

16,000 staff from all members. The civil services for all UN organizations. Prepares reports, statistics, budgets etc.

54 members, elected by General Assembly. Meets twice a year. Supervises the many specialized agencies and commissions. Works through six functional commissions, five regional commissions, eight standing committees and various groups of experts.

159 members. Meets annually. Debates any issue. Six major committees. Resolutions (not binding) with two-thirds majority. Elects Secretary-General and judges in International Court. Votes UN budget. Helps supervise and select members of other UN bodies.

Fifteen members (five permanent and ten elected for two years). Main UN peace-keeping organization. Can order cease-fires, negotiate, impose sanctions and intervene with force. Permanent members have a veto on decisions. Nominates Secretary-General. Votes for judges in International Court.

Specialized international organizations include:
FAO
(Food and Agriculture Organization of the United Nations)
IDA
(International Development Association)
ILO
(International Labour Organisation)
IMF
(International Monetary Fund)
IMO
(International Maritime Organization)
UNESCO
(United Nations Educational Scientific and Cultural Organization)
WFP
(Joint UN/FAO World Food Programme)
WHO
(World Health Organization)
WMO
(World Meteorological Organization)

Organizations include:
IAEA
(International Atomic Energy Agency)

UN Forces include:
UNDOF
(United Nations Disengagement Observer Force)
UNFICYP
(United Nations Peacekeeping Force in Cyprus)
UNIFIL
(United Nations Interim Force in Lebanon)
UNMOGIP
(United Nations Military Observer Group in India and Pakistan)

INSTRAW
(International Research and Training Institute for the Advancement of Women)
UNHCR
(Office of the United Nations High Commissioner for Refugees)
UNICEF
(United Nations Children's Fund)
UNRWA
(United Nations Relief and Works Agency for Palestine Refugees in the Near East)
UNU
(United Nations University)

Disarmament Commission

The peacekeepers

The prime function of the United Nations is to preserve world peace. Given the huge stockpiles of nuclear weapons throughout the world, and the international threat these pose, keeping world peace is perhaps an impossible responsibility for the UN.

The branch of the UN primarily responsible for the maintenance of international peace is the Security Council. This Council has five permanent members: Britain, China, France, the United States and the USSR. It has sometimes been questioned whether Britain and France should still be on the Council. Major Security Council decisions have to be agreed by all five permanent members, thus giving any one of them a form of veto if they abstain or vote against the motion.

In 1950 the USSR walked out of the Council in protest when China's seat was given to the nationalist government in Taiwan, rather than the communists in Peking. This enabled the Council to take the only positive action it has ever taken, over Korea (see page 22). When the Soviets returned, the Assembly passed a special resolution that enabled it to meet when the Security Council was deadlocked and, if necessary, recommend the use of force. This procedure, known as "Uniting for Peace," has been attempted once or twice but its legality has not been established.

This cartoon, entitled "History doesn't repeat itself," was published at the end of June 1950, when UN forces were being moved into Korea.

◄This unanimous vote of the Security Council in 1949 was to approve a full meeting of the General Assembly to discuss the crisis in the Middle East. The Lebanonese (upper left) could not vote.

►The Security Council meeting in emergency session during the Cuban missile crisis in 1962. The UN Secretary-General was U Thant.

Originally the "big five" were joined by six non-permanent members, elected to the Council for two years. In 1963 their number was increased to ten, with five from Asia and Africa. It is questionable whether a Security Council on which the major powers can be outvoted two-to-one is an effective organization for preserving world peace.

Consider the cartoon on the facing page. It seems to suggest that the United Nations would succeed where the League of Nations had failed. The UN, like the League, can investigate a conflict, call for a ceasefire and impose sanctions against an aggressor. It can investigate situations that might get out of hand, and suggest ways in which they might be defused. Most important, however, the Security Council can call on member countries to provide troops for UN forces. These can either act as peacekeepers, or even give military support to a country unjustly attacked. Only once has this last course of action been taken, in Korea in 1950. In most instances, the Security Council has not been able to agree to order the active use of UN forces.

Toward a better world

In 1975 the General Assembly met in a special session to debate poverty in Africa. This cartoon is from the London *Sunday Telegraph*.

The Preamble to the Charter of the United Nations states that one of its main aims is "to promote social progress and better standards of life in larger freedom," and "to employ international machinery for the promotion of the economic and social advancement of all peoples." In this field the United Nations has been tireless in its efforts and has achieved a very great deal.

The chief agency for coordinating the economic and social work of the UN and the organizations that work with it is the Economic and Social Council. The Council's fifty-four members are divided into three equal groups of eighteen. One group is elected by the General Assembly every three years. The Council meets in both New York and Geneva.

The work of the Council is done through two groups of organizations. You can see these in the diagram on page 13. The first group is made up of agencies set up by the United Nations itself. One of the most famous of these is the United Nations Children's Fund (UNICEF). UNICEF Christmas cards are well known and help to raise money and publicize the Fund's work. The Council's supervision of these agencies is shared with the General Assembly.

The majority of the second group of agencies are not so directly related to the UN, but are included in what is known as the "United Nations family" of organizations. These include the International Monetary Fund, the World Bank and the World Health Organization.

In order to help it in its massive tasks of coordinating, funding and initiating the work of its agencies, the Council is served by four separate groups. These comprise:

1 Eight Standing Committees, which cover matters such as Natural Resources.
2 Six Functional Commissions, which deal with issues such as Human Rights or Population.
3 Five Regional Commissions, such as the Economic Commission for Latin America.
4 A number of expert bodies, for example, the Committee on Crime Prevention and Control.

All these commissions, agencies and other groups might seem rather dull and bureaucratic, but many people would argue that their work does more to promote international understanding and peace than the Security Council.

Finally, there is a Trusteeship Council. This was established to keep an eye on the administration of certain former colonies before they achieved independence. Of the eleven territories originally held, only the Trust Territory of Pacific Islands remains in a state of dependancy.

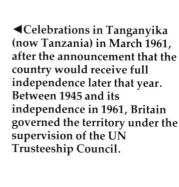

▲UNICEF is one of the many relief agencies working in refugee camps, such as this one for Kampucheans on the Thai border.

◄Celebrations in Tanganyika (now Tanzania) in March 1961, after the announcement that the country would receive full independence later that year. Between 1945 and its independence in 1961, Britain governed the territory under the supervision of the UN Trusteeship Council.

Running the UN

1 The Secretariat

More than 16,000 men and women from over 140 nations work for the UN Secretariat. They are employed in New York, Geneva, Vienna, and in countless offices and fieldwork centers throughout the world. Apart from the Secretary-General, the most powerful are Under-Secretaries-General who run whole departments. Below them spreads a confusing network of administrators, experts in almost any field you care to name (from bee-keeping to ballistic missiles), advisers, clerks, translators, secretaries, guides and guards.

Considering its size and unique responsibilities, the system works well. But there are problems:

- Recruitment. UN staff have to be very able; and they also have to come from as wide a geographical area as possible. It is sometimes difficult to fulfill both of these requirements.
- Unlike the U.S. Civil Service, which is supervised by Congress and an elected government, there is no similar body to keep a check on the UN Secretariat.
- There is a tendency in the UN to set up more and more committees, departments and programs. This increased bureaucracy can lead to less and less action. Effective international action continues to be very difficult to organize.

2 The Secretary-General

The first Secretary-General of the UN described his task as "the most impossible job in the world."[10] A recent writer explained:

> It is almost impossible for him [the Secretary-General] to appear right in the eyes of the UN members . . . He must be politician, diplomatist and civil servant in one. It is thus an office that is impossible to fulfill to the satisfaction of all.[11]

The Secretary-General has plenty of responsibility, but little power. The UN Charter states that he is the Chief Administrative Officer of the UN. It empowers him to make an annual report to the General Assembly; to "bring to the attention of the Security Council any matter which, in his opinion, may threaten . . . international peace and security"; and to "use his good offices to help in resolving international disputes."[12] Secretary General Kurt Waldheim said his job had been "splendid misery."[13]

Lucille Mair of Jamaica, who became a UN Under-Secretary-General when she was put in charge of an International Conference on the Question of Palestine.

The controversial Austrian president, Kurt Waldheim, who became the UN Secretary-General in 1972. When he retired in 1982 he described the job as "impossible."

3 The Budget

The UN and its agencies spend over $54 billion a year. Almost ninety percent of this goes into economic, social and humanitarian activities. In 1984, for example, the World Health Organization spent about $490 million. There are three main problems with the UN's massive budget: how is it to be raised, what is it to be spent on, and who ensures that it is spent efficiently. There is much argument over the last two problems, but how the money is raised is more difficult. Examine the table below. In each column the countries listed are those that contribute the most under that heading. Although the major Western powers appear to contribute the most according to the left-hand column, their contributions are a very small percentage of their national income and none of these countries appear in the other columns. This would not seem to be the fairest possible manner of raising funds.

Total contribution to the UN system (in millions of dollars)		$ contributed per head of population		Contributions as a percentage of a country's national income	
United States	950·8	Norway	34·73	Gambia	0·596
Japan	361·4	Denmark	21·94	Equatorial Guinea	0·438
West Germany	252·8	Sweden	19·05	Comoros	0·372
Italy	177·3	Qatar	18·33	Uganda	0·356
Canada	174·5	Netherlands	10·21	Guinea-Bissau	0·334
Britain	169·9	Saudi Arabia	9·46	Norway	0·319

(All figures are for 1984).[14]

International justice

It has long been the dream of mankind to be able to settle disputes between nations in court, rather than on the battlefield. During the last century it was not uncommon for a third party, an arbitrator, to be called in to mediate between nations. In 1899 a Permanent Court of Arbitration was set up, and when the League of Nations was established in 1919 an International Court of Justice was founded, too. This Court was re-established, as part of the United Nations system, in 1945.

The Court of fifteen judges meets at The Hague, in Holland. The judges, who are elected by the General Assembly and the Security Council, represent all the major legal systems of the world. There may not be more than one judge from a country. If the Court needs to make a quick judgement only five judges sit, but this has not been necessary to date.

An international court to settle disputes between nations is a fine idea, but it faces considerable practical problems. First, only about 45 of the 159 UN members are prepared to accept the Court's authority, so most disputes never get to the Court, and even when they do, nations that would normally accept the Court's ruling sometimes refuse to do so. In 1984, for example, the United States declared that it would not abide by the rulings of the Court in cases

The Peace Palace in The Hague in Holland, headquarters for the International Court of Justice.

In 1969 the International Court of Justice made a ruling on how the dispute between West Germany, Denmark and Holland over oil-drilling rights in the North Sea might be settled. Unfortunately, the Court is only rarely effective as an arbitrator.

involving Central America. The Court makes rulings at a rate of less than one a year.

Second, once the Court has made a ruling, who will enforce it? For example, if the French courts make a ruling, the French police make sure that it is carried out, but there are no UN police to support UN judgements. In 1971 the Court ruled that South Africa had no legal right to be in Namibia, a territory that it had looked after as a mandate for the League of Nations, but the South African government was not obliged to obey the words of fifteen judges on the other side of the world. The Court is not always ignored, however. For example, in 1953 France accepted the Court's ruling that certain of the Channel Islands were British.

Finally, what law is the Court supposed to enforce? It can uphold customs and conventions, but despite the work of the International Law Commission, international law is unclear and not widely accepted. A similar body, the UN Commission on International Trade Law, tries to establish principles for harmonious international trade. In spite of the UN's efforts, therefore, the world is a very long way from enjoying an international system of law.

3
CASE STUDIES
Korea

ALTHOUGH THE USSR AND the United States were allies during World War II, they were deeply suspicious of each other, and were divided by their different political ideologies, communism and capitalism. By 1949 relations between the two superpowers were so bad that many feared the outbreak of a third World War. In 1945, at the end of World War II, the Soviets had liberated North Korea, the Americans South Korea. Korea was divided between communists in the north and a pro-United States republic in the south. A United Nations Commission was set up to solve the Korean problem, but it had no power to make demands on the Americans and Soviets. In the end, however, the foreign powers withdrew their forces, leaving Korea divided at the 38th parallel. Then, on June 25, 1950, news reached the headquarters of the UN that communist North Korea had attacked the Republic of Korea in the south. This was the UN's first major test.

The Security Council met at once and ordered a ceasefire. When this failed, the Council recommended to all members of the

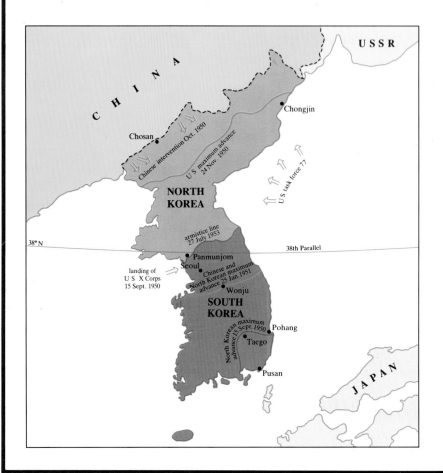

The Korean peninsula, the only part of the world in which UN forces have played an active military role in trying to bring about peace. The country remains divided at the 38th parallel.

UN that they

> . . . furnish such assistance to the Republic of Korea as might be necessary to repel the armed attack and restore international peace and security in the area.[15]

The bulk of the UN forces in Korea were American. The United States lost 142,000 men, compared with 17,000 lost by other UN countries. The UN was pleased to release this Korean photograph, showing its military police from several nations.

Sixteen nations sent troops and five sent medical teams. The United States was empowered by the Security Council to command UN forces. By October the North Koreans had been driven back over the 38th parallel. At first glance it seemed as if the UN action had been an outstanding success. The reality, however, was different.

The Security Council supported aggressive UN action for a number of reasons which relate to its various members. The United States, Britain and France are democratic countries opposed to communism and therefore supported South Korea. By 1949 communists had seized control of all mainland China, but the seat on the Security Council was still held by the nationalists who were in exile on the island of Taiwan. Naturally, they supported South Korea. The Soviets did not veto the UN action, because they were boycotting the Security Council in protest at the decision not to give China's seat to the communists. In light of this, it is hard to say whether UN support for South Korea truly reflected the UN sentiments.

U.S. General Douglas MacArthur, who commanded the UN forces, did not stop at the 38th parallel, but went on into North Korea and wanted to attack China. The Chinese communists then joined in the fighting, which continued until 1953.

Korea is still divided at the 38th parallel. So-called UN forces remain in South Korea. Brian Urquhart, the author of *Hammarskjöld,* wrote that by 1953 UN "morale fell to its lowest level."[16]

Israel and Palestine

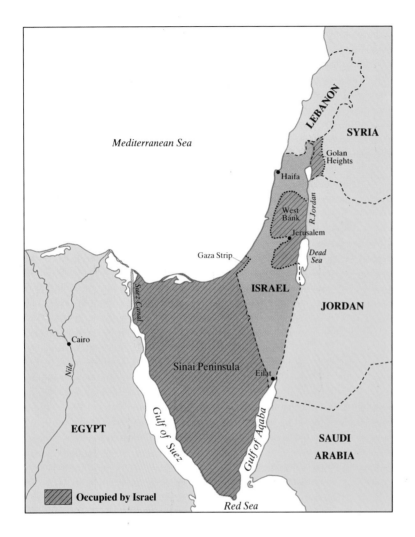

A map of Israel, showing the area taken over in 1948 (in green), and the territory occupied by Israel in 1967. The map shows quite clearly why, for military reasons, Israel is so anxious to remain in the territory known as the West Bank. Without it Israel's waist is very thin, making the country vulnerable.

The dispute over Palestine (now Israel) is essentially quite simple, although the solution is not. Two peoples, the Jews and the Palestinian Arabs, claim the same territory as their homeland.

At the end of World War I, Palestine was made a League of Nations mandate under British care. In the period between the wars there was an enormous increase in Jewish immigration into Palestine, and conflicting interests and expectations led to trouble between the Jews and the Palestinian Arabs. By 1947, unable to cope with the problems of maintaining control in the mandated territory, Britain appealed for help from the UN, announcing it was going to withdraw from Palestine. The UN voted to partition Palestine into Jewish and Arab states. Even before the British had left, however, Jewish forces began to take control of as much territory as they could, forcing 300,000 Palestinians to flee. On May 15, 1948, the British officially left and the State of Israel – already at war with its Arab neighbors – was declared. Throughout the Arab–Israeli conflict the United Nations has made various attempts to achieve peace, as shown in the table opposite.

There seem to be two main reasons why the UN has found it so difficult to act effectively over the Arab–Israeli problem. The first is the attitudes of the two parties involved. The Proclamation of the Independence of the State of Israel, 1948, stated:

The land of Israel was the birthplace of the Jewish people. Here their spiritual, religious and national identity was formed.[17]

In direct opposition to this, Yasser Arafat, the leader of the Palestine Liberation Organization, said in 1983: "the struggle will continue until . . . the establishment of our independent Palestinian state."[18] Neither side was willing to abandon its claim.

The second reason lies in the attitude of the superpowers. In May 1967, a Russian, Marshal Gretchko, said in Egypt:

The USSR, her armed forces, her people and Government will stand by the Arabs and will continue to encourage and support them.[19]

The United States, on the other hand, has tended to side with Israel. When things were going badly for Israel at the start of the 1973 war, President Nixon stated: "We will not let Israel go down the tubes. We [will] replace all their losses."[20] It is difficult for the UN to act if the superpowers disagree.

	Event	*UN Action*
1947	British wish to leave Palestine. Fighting in Palestine.	General Assembly proposal to partition Palestine between Jews and Arabs.
1948–49	War between Israel and the Palestinians, supported by Egypt, Jordan, Syria and Lebanon.	Security Council calls for truce. Count Bernadotte appointed UN mediator. UN Truce Supervision Organization (UNTSO) established.
1949	Uneasy peace.	UN Relief and Works Agency for Palestinian Refugees established. UNTSO supervises the peace.
1956	Israel, Britain and France invade Egypt to seize Suez Canal.	General Assembly calls for ceasefire and sends in UN Emergency Force (UNEF). UN clears Suez Canal and UNEF, based on Egyptian soil, acts as a buffer between Egyptian and Israeli forces.
May 1967		UNEF withdrawn at Egypt's request.
June 1967	Six-Day War, between Egypt, Jordan, Syria and Israel. Israel occupies Gaza Strip, Golan Heights, West Bank, Sinai.	Security Council calls for ceasefire. Security Council Resolution 242 sets out basis for lasting peace in the area.
1973	Syria and Egypt attack Israel.	Security Council calls for ceasefire. UN Peace Conference established at Geneva. A new UNEF sent to Sinai.
1974	Hostilities finally cease.	A UN observer force set up on Israeli–Syrian border.
1978		UN peacekeeping force set up along Israeli–Lebanon border.
1979	Camp David Peace Treaty.	
1982	Israel invades Lebanon. Fighting in and around Beirut.	UN forces swept aside. Numerous resolutions and initiatives for peace. UN observer force remains in Lebanon.
1985	Israeli forces withdraw. Serious civil disturbances continue in Lebanon.	
1987–88	Palestinian riots on West Bank and in Gaza Strip.	

Cyprus

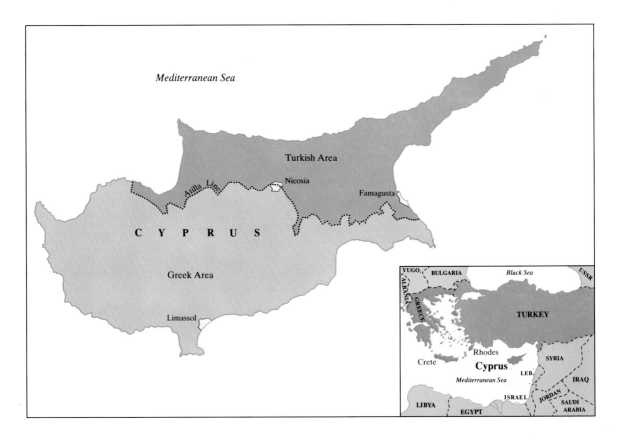

The island of Cyprus in the eastern Mediterranean has been termed the "orphan child of the United Nations."[21] Since 1964 the United Nations has been the only element of stability in this strife-torn island.

As in Palestine, the problem in Cyprus is one of competing peoples. Of the island's population of 650,000 in the early 1960s, four-fifths were Greek Cypriots. They were members of the Greek Orthodox Christian Church, spoke Greek and identified closely with Greek customs and traditions. The remaining 130,000 were Turkish Cypriots. They were Turkish-speaking Muslims who looked to Turkey for leadership. The Turkish mainland is only forty miles away.

Between 1878 and 1960 Cyprus was governed by Britain, and the two groups on the island lived in relative harmony. During the

The divided Mediterranean island of Cyprus. The presence of a UN peacekeeping force between the Turkish and Greek sectors has helped to stabilize the uneasy situation that has existed since 1964.

1950s Cypriots of both groups forced the British to end their colonial rule, and the island became independent in 1960. Already there had been signs of tension between the two groups of Cypriots. With the British gone, the situation deteriorated quickly. Fighting broke out, and in 1963 Archbishop Makarios, president of Cyprus, invited British troops back, but they were too unpopular to be successful. In 1964 the UN was invited to help settle the problem.

Not surprisingly, the United Nations could not find an instant answer to Cyprus's troubles. The Security Council acted quite rapidly and, in March 1964, the lightly armed UN Force in Cyprus (UNFICYP), comprising troops from Canada, Denmark, Sweden, Finland and Ireland, arrived to act as a buffer between the two groups. Nevertheless, sporadic violence continued, and in 1974 forces from the Turkish mainland occupied northern Cyprus after fierce fighting. The UNFICYP was powerless to stop them. In 1983 northern Cyprus declared itself to be the Turkish Republic of Northern Cyprus. The island remains divided to this day.

Has the UN failed? A modern historian has written:

There is an erroneous view that . . . UN peacekeeping is completely ineffective. With one hand tied behind its back, this argument goes, UN peacekeeping only "works" when it is not needed. When the chips are really down, as . . . in Cyprus at the time of the Turkish invasion in 1974 . . . UN forces either withdraw or are contemptuously brushed aside. But quite apart from ignoring the fact the UNFICYP possibly broke up the momentum of the Turkish advance into Cyprus, this overlooks the invaluable work . . . which UN forces do in reducing the mayhem created by violent groups . . . More seriously still, however, it mistakes the principal function of UN peacekeeping altogether – which is not so much to prevent wars between states as to help consolidate their termination. [22]

Perhaps the situation in Cyprus would have been worse without the UN presence.

Turkish Cypriot guerrilla soldiers. A careful look at the terrain in which the men are fighting shows why it is well suited to guerrilla tactics.

Congo/Zaïre

Indian troops, serving with the UN in the Congo in 1962, face a crowd of angry Katangese. The UN believed that in Africa in the 1960s Indian troops would arouse less hostility than Europeans.

Between 1960 and 1964 the United Nations engaged in a successful peacekeeping operation in the Congo. Despite the success, the UN was criticized, and member states quarreled bitterly over its action. The whole episode is a good example of the strengths and weaknesses of the organization.

The Congo was a large Belgian colony in central Africa, rich in diamonds and valuable metals. It became independent in June 1960, but almost at once it was plunged into chaos. There were widespread anti-white riots and the Belgians, who now had no legal right over the country, flew in paratroopers to protect the Europeans. The Belgian action only made the situation worse. At the same time in southern Congo the province of Katanga declared itself independent. The president and prime minister of the Republic of the Congo asked the UN for help.

With unusual speed the Security Council met and voted to give the Congo

> . . . such military assistance as may be necessary until through the efforts of the Congolese Government, with the technical assistance of the United Nations, the national security forces may be able . . . to meet fully their tasks.[23]

Within two days the first contingents of a United Nations Force (ONUC) were arriving

28

in the Congo. One might ask how the UN had managed to act so swiftly.

The USSR backed the resolution because it seemed to be hostile to Belgium, a Western ally. In general, Western nations also supported the resolution because it seemed an effective way of avoiding slaughter in the Congo. China, France and Britain abstained. In other words, the nations of the UN took rapid action as much because they wished to further their own ends, as to see the Congo helped.

The same interests that launched the ONUC also hampered its effectiveness. The Soviet leader Nikita Khrushchev soon denounced the ONUC and the UN Secretary-General Dag Hammarskjöld, accusing the Western colonial powers of "doing their dirty-work in the Congo through the Secretary-

General of the United Nations and his staff . . ."[24] The question of whether a Secretary-General can ever be completely unbiased is, of course, an insoluble problem for the UN. The USSR vetoed several Security Council resolutions and refused to pay for the ONUC. It claimed that the UN was interfering in the internal affairs of a member country.

The fighting continued for three years. The UN gradually helped to defeat the rebels and rebuild the shattered country – the modern Zaïre. Whether UN forces should have been used is still an open question.

Doctors working in the Congo for the World Health Organization. The WHO is one of the most effective and respected of the UN's special agencies.

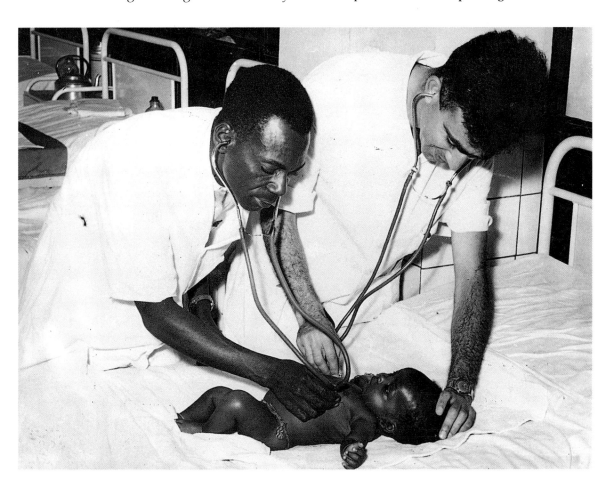

Kashmir

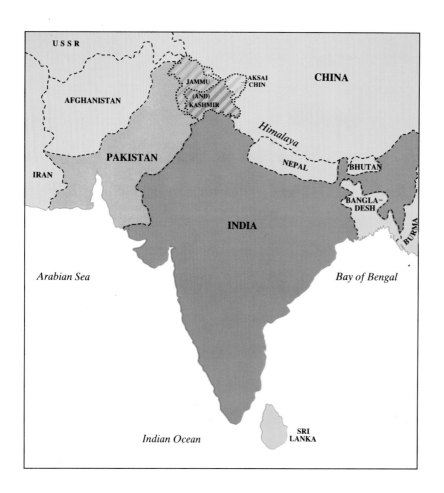

▶UN observers on the India–Pakistan border sorting out the problem of Pakistani cattle that had wandered across the cease-fire line. Without the presence of the UN, such an innocent event might have led to further bloodshed.

◀A map showing the disputed Kashmir area between India and Pakistan, where the UN has had observers since 1948.

A quick glance at the map above will reveal just why the Indian province of Kashmir is such a strategically important area: it has frontiers with two superpowers, as well as with Afghanistan and Pakistan. It is not surprising, therefore, that when India and Pakistan became separate countries in 1947, Kashmir was a disputed territory. The situation was made worse by the fact that Kashmir, which joined Hindu India, was largely populated by Muslims, supported by Pakistan. An outline of the conflict is given in the box on the facing page.

In trying to solve the Kashmir problem the Security Council has used many of the powers at its disposal.

- An appeal for a ceasefire (1965).

- Conciliation between the two opposing sides (1949–50).
- Trying to find out the facts behind a dispute (1948).
- Sending observers to act as a buffer between two hostile groups (1949 onward).
- Stating clearly what the answer to a dispute is. The Council has refrained from doing this too forcefully in Kashmir, but it has made it clear that it thinks an answer to the problem is to allow the people of Kashmir to decide the future of their country for themselves in a plebiscite. So far, India has prevented this.

The Security Council has not sent in an armed peacekeeping force. Nor has there been active military intervention on

▲Pakistani refugees in an Indian camp after an outbreak of fighting in Kashmir in 1971. As in all wars, it is the civilians caught in the conflict who suffer most.

behalf of either party. The UN has attempted this only in Korea.

Some members of the UN feel that the Security Council's peacekeeping efforts in Kasmir have been inadequate. However, as in other disputes, the powers of the UN are limited.

Date	Event
Pre-1947	Kashmir under the hereditary rule of a Hindu Maharajah, subject to Britain.
Aug. 1947	India and Pakistan gain independence from Britain as separate states.
Oct. 1947	Kashmir joins India; fighting along border with Pakistan.
1948	Security Council establishes a UN Commission for India and Pakistan to investigate and mediate.
Jan. 1949	UN ceasefire comes into effect, supervised by UN observers and mediators.
1957	Kashmir formally part of Indian Union.
1965	Hostilities renewed, ceasefire again arranged by UN, with observers to uphold it.
1966	UN supervises troop withdrawal.
1971	More fighting, ending in another UN ceasefire.
1972	India and Pakistan agree on a "line of control" supervised by the UN, but the dispute over Kashmir remains unsettled.

Iran and Iraq

In the long and bitter Iran–Iraq War (1980–88), the UN's ability to take effective action was limited by the same factors that handicapped it in other conflicts. The need for the support of all the superpowers, for both sides in the conflict to agree to abide by UN mediation, for both sides to want peace, and simply for the UN to be called in before the conflict has gone too far – these difficult conditions have repeatedly restricted the UN's powers as a peacekeeping organization.

Escalating clashes in Iran–Iraq border areas in 1980 led to the Iraqi invasion of Iranian territory in September 1980. The reasons for the attack had largely to do with a long-standing dispute over control of the strategically and economically important Shatt al Arab waterway, but there was also tension as a result of their different political and religious systems and their new leaders – the Ayatollah Khomeini in Iran, and Saddam Hussein in Iraq.

Iraq was much better equipped, but Iran, with a population three times the size of Iraq's, had the advantage of numbers. The battles were costly to both sides, and by 1982 Iraq's economy was under a terrible strain. In June 1982 Iraq declared a withdrawal from Iran, but Iran did not stop fighting. Not content with expelling the Iraqis, the Iranians wanted to punish Saddam Hussein and his government, and to claim reparations. Iran now took the offensive and attacked Iraqi territory where the fighting

U.S. Navy minesweepers in the Persian Gulf in 1987. It might have been better if such vessels had operated under the UN flag.

continued, with little advance either way, for the next five years.

The oil wealth of the Persian Gulf makes it an area of strategic importance to many countries, and this partially accounts for the Iran–Iraq War being of particular international concern. By 1987 the focus of the Iran–Iraq War had shifted from land to the waters of the Gulf and the so-called tanker war. The superpowers now became more actively involved as they responded to Kuwait's plea for protection from Iranian attacks on its shipping. The USSR and the United States responded by providing Kuwait with naval escorts; neither wanted the other to gain influence in the area. Western European countries were reluctant to become involved, but as shipping began to be endangered outside the Persian Gulf, Britain, France, Italy, The Netherlands and Belgium all sent minesweepers and warships to protect their oil supplies.

The greatest hope for a settlement of the Iran–Iraq War seemed to lie with the UN. The first resolution passed by the Security Council on September 18, 1980, calling for a ceasefire (but not for the withdrawal of Iraqi troops from Iran), had no effect – other than to inspire the Iranian claim that the UN was biased toward Iraq. The UN Secretary-General, Javier Pérez de Cuéllar, managed to negotiate a temporary ceasefire on civilian targets in June 1984, but a general peace initiative in April 1985 failed. In 1987, mounting anxiety over the tanker war led to another Security Council meeting and something of a breakthrough. The five permanent members – Britain, China, France, the United States, and the USSR – all voted for a compulsory resolution.

Resolution 598 carried with it the possibility of sanctions against whichever party did not accept it. The resolution called for a ceasefire, a withdrawal of forces, the exchange of prisoners, and, with an inquiry into responsibility for the conflict (designed to appease Iran), mediation on a permanent settlement. It also condemned the use of

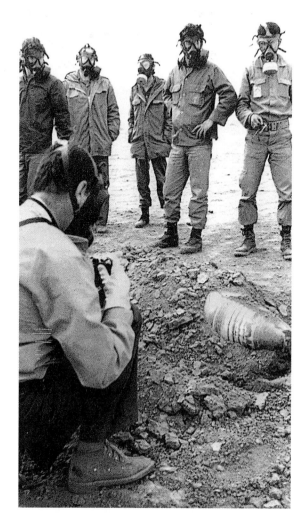

Although both sides denied their use, the UN proved that chemical weapons were employed during the Iran–Iraq War. A member of a UN fact-finding delegation is shown here examining an unexploded Iraqi chemical bomb.

chemical weapons. Iraq accepted the resolution immediately, and although at first Iran would not agree to a ceasefire unless Iraq was officially declared the aggressor, eventually Iran too agreed to the ceasefire. The UN's successful mediation in the Gulf War, led by Javier Pérez de Cuéllar, is generally recognized as one of the UN's outstanding achievements.

Disarmament

This cartoon is entitled "Guy Fawkes 1946." Guy Fawkes tried to blow up the British Parliament with gunpowder in 1605. The cartoonist shows the atom bomb as the new equivalent to Guy Fawkes. What is threatened is civilization, not just Parliament.

When the Covenant of the League of Nations was written in 1919 it called for a general reduction in armaments throughout the world. At the time when Hitler came to power in Germany, a major Disarmament Conference was in session at Geneva. Hitler withdrew the German delegation, the conference collapsed, and the world moved steadily toward war.

Although there was a general desire in 1945 never to allow war to devastate the world again, the United Nations was more realistic than the League about how to achieve peace. The Charter talked only of the "regulation of armaments." The cartoon above indicates why, in the years that followed, the UN gradually moved away from a policy of controlling armaments to one of disarmament. The cartoon shows the British Parliamentary guards discovering not Guy Fawkes (who planned to blow up Parliament with gunpowder in 1605), but a much more horrifying threat. What is at stake is not just the Houses of Parliament, as you can see from the writing on the roof.

In 1959 the General Assembly agreed on an aim of "general and complete disarmament." The 1970s was declared a "Decade of Disarmament," although very little was achieved, and the 1980s was given the same title. There were two General Assembly Special Sessions on disarmament, in 1978 and in 1982, but still the stockpiles of weapons around the world, both nuclear and conventional, have continued to grow. Two questions need to be answered:

1 Has the UN achieved anything in the field of disarmament?
- The UN had supervised numerous arms limitation treaties, such as the 1959 Antarctic Treaty, banning nuclear weapons from that continent. The principle has now been extended to outer space (1966), Latin America (1967), and the ocean bed (1970). Other treaties have helped limit chemical and biological weapons (1971), and the spread of nuclear weapons (1968).
- The UN has also kept the issue of disarmament before the world, although the SALT negotiations in 1972 and 1979, and the 1987 INF Treaty were the result of a superpowers' initiative and were not held under the auspices of the UN.

2 Why has the United Nations not been more successful in furthering disarmament? Evan Luard, a historian of the UN, offers four reasons why the superpowers are so unwilling to disarm:

- The risk involved, particularly for the generals.
- The lack of trust on either side.
- The ghastly consequences if one side were to violate an agreement.
- The problem of balancing different types of weapons.[25]

So, although the UN can urge arms control, "the key to its solution is in the hands of the two major nuclear powers."[26]

▲Khrushchev speaking after the signing of the Nuclear Test Ban Treaty in August 1963. UN Secretary-General U Thant, standing behind Khrushchev, witnessed the signing.

◄Reagan and Gorbachev negotiated the 1987 INF Treaty with little reference to the UN. The most significant disarmament achievements of the 1980s were independent of the UN.

4
HUMAN RIGHTS
Repressive regimes

ON DECEMBER 10, 1948, the United Nations adopted a Universal Declaration of Human Rights:

> *Whereas recognition of the inherent dignity and of the equal and inalienable rights of all members of the human family is the foundation of freedom, justice and peace in the world . . . the General Assembly proclaims this Universal Declaration of Human Rights as the common standard of achievement for all peoples and nations.*

There then follows a comprehensive list of human rights. They include the right to life, liberty and security of person; freedom from slavery; freedom from torture or degrading punishment; the right to equal protection of the law; the right to privacy; freedom of movement; freedom of conscience and of religion; the right of assembly; and the right to take part in government. To these are added other entitlements, such as the right to work, to rest, to education, and to an adequate standard of health and living. All these rights are equal to all, without distinction on account of race, sex, language or religion.

Soviet tanks in the Czechoslovakian capital Prague in the summer of 1968. The Soviets overturned a legitimate government because they considered it dangerously liberal, infringing on the people's right of self-determination. Unfortunately, the UN was unable to stop them.

A poster drawing attention to the plight of prisoners held by repressive regimes worldwide.

These concepts are almost universally recognized as extremely worthy. But now consider clause 7 of article 2 of the UN Charter:

> *Nothing contained in the present Charter shall authorize the United Nations to intervene in matters which are essentially within the domestic jurisdiction of any state.*

There is, of course, a contradiction here. In the end a declaration of rights is only words on paper. The UN cannot force a state to change its ways.

The UN can, however, create a tide of world opinion that can help oppressed people. In recent years its Commission on Human Rights has looked into abuses of human rights in Chile, Poland, Palestine (Israel), Afghanistan, El Salvador, Guatemala, Iran, Kampuchea and South Africa.

Governments do not like to be shown up as cruel or harsh before the world. Kurt Waldheim wrote in 1980:

> *. . . we have not failed altogether. Since the adoption of the Universal Declaration of Human Rights in December 1948, the principles that it sets forth have been incorporated into the constitutions of many new states and have unquestioningly been a positive influence on international ethics.*[27]

Here are some ways in which the UN might try to protect human rights more effectively:
- Arranging economic sanctions against regimes that infringe on human rights.
- Sending in UN forces to protect groups or individuals who are deprived of basic human rights.
- Publishing worldwide details of cases in which human rights have been infringed.

Some, if not all, of these proposals might be practicable.

Apartheid

The first two articles of the Universal Declaration of Human Rights begin:

> 1 *All human beings are born free and equal in dignity and rights. They are endowed with reason and conscience, and should act toward one another in a spirit of brotherhood.*
> 2 *Everyone is entitled to all the rights and freedoms set forth in this declaration, without distinction of any kind, such as race, color . . .*

In South Africa, however, a different set of values has been in force since 1948: "Total segregation should not only be the ideal, but the immediate practical policy of the State."[28] Blacks, who make up the great majority of the population, have been moved into "homelands," separate from white areas. The blacks may not participate in the government of South Africa, and their separate facilities are everywhere inferior to those for whites. For example, in 1985 UNESCO estimated that in South Africa a white child has more than twelve times as much spent on his or her education as a black child.

Clearly the policies of the South African government run against the Declaration of Human Rights. They also run contrary to the whole spirit of the United Nations, which seeks to bring people all over the world closer together, not separate or segregate them. In some ways apartheid seems worse than other breaches of human rights. The policy of "separate development" (as apartheid is alternatively known) condemns people for what they are rather than for what they have done. In the USSR dissidents have been imprisoned without fair trial for what they have written, but in South Africa people are denied rights just because they are born black.

To counter apartheid the UN has taken various steps:

An anti-apartheid demonstration in London in 1987. The slogan is "Sanctions Now."

- A Special Committee Against Apartheid has been set up.
- The General Assembly has established the UN Trust Fund for South Africa.
- The Security Council has demanded an arms embargo on South Africa.
- The General Assembly has called for all countries to boycott South African goods and break off diplomatic relations with South Africa.
- International publicity has been given to the injustice of the apartheid system, and South Africa has been condemned in numerous UN resolutions.

But apartheid remains, a vivid example of how difficult the UN finds it to persuade its member states ever to agree or act on a single policy. Consider the strategic importance of South Africa's position at the southern tip of Africa. Here, as in other areas, the superpowers' competition for influence has affected their support for UN resolutions. Some people believe that Western governments have been unprepared to press the right-wing South African government too hard for fear that it might help to bring communist groups to power.

Apartheid in South Africa. The UN is unable to interfere in a country's internal affairs.

5
WELFARE
Food and population

THE PICTURE OPPOSITE SHOWS famine victims in Africa. The photograph below shows something of the huge quantities of grain available in the West. The stark contrast between these two scenes illustrates one of the main reasons for the existence of the United Nations. There is enough food being produced in the world at the moment for everyone to be fed adequately. However, in the richer nations some people die because they eat too much, while famine claims hundreds of thousands of victims in the poorer countries. The response of the UN to this shameful contrast is twofold. It encourages the richer nations to share their wealth and food with less fortunate peoples and it seeks to "promote higher standards of living, full employment and conditions of economic and social progress and development" in what are termed the Third World countries.[29]

The work of the United Nations for human welfare has been much more spectacular and successful than that for the prevention of war. The largest section of the UN's budget is devoted to achieving economic and social progress: it allocated $503,404,800 for the year 1984–85.

The immediate work of the UN is concerned with famine relief. In 1972 a United Nations Disaster Relief Coordinator (UNDRU) was established, with an office in Geneva. UNDRU has three functions:

- To gather and pass on information about disaster areas.
- To organize relief missions.

A grain mountain. Overproduction of foodstuffs is a real problem confronting the sophisticated agricultural industries in the West.

Millions of people in the Third World, like these Ethiopian refugees, are seriously undernourished.

● To help governments avoid the recurrence of disasters.

The long-term aim of the UN is to ensure that the need for emergency food supplies gets less and less. With this end in mind a UN World Food Conference met in Rome in 1974, leading to the foundation of the World Food Council (WFC). The Council helps countries plan their future food needs, and shows them how they can set about achieving self-sufficiency. Other Agencies working under the UN are the Food and Agriculture Organization, and the International Fund for Agricultural Development.

Consider these statistics:

	1950	1960	1970	1980	2000
World population (billions)	2.5	3	3.6	4.7	7.3 (estimated)

It is alarming to realize how large world population may be by 2050. Through its Fund for Population Activities (UNFPA) the UN tries to help countries bring their populations under control with family planning programs and other related aid. Work such as that being done by UNFPA is essential to control population growth.

Health

Most young people in the West take good health for granted. They are not sick very often, and when they are, effective treatment is usually available. Britons, for example, are proud of their National Health Service; many see access to medical treatment as a fundamental right. Unfortunately, in many parts of the world this is not the case. But, largely through the World Health Organization, the United Nations is seeking to extend to everyone "the highest possible level of health."[30]

Founded in 1948, the World Health Organization (WHO) is the second largest of the intergovernmental agencies that work with the UN through its Economic and Social Council. In 1984 it had a staff of 5,329 and a budget of $490,350,000. Obviously the health of a country's people is the responsibility of its government, and the WHO cannot enter or aid a state unless it has the cooperation of the local authorities; but disease knows no frontiers. All countries, especially those in the Third World with several frontiers, realize that they must work together to overcome their problems. This is one area where the WHO can help.

Much of the WHO's time and money is spent on international matters, which can be divided into four categories: research, coordination of programs, writing reports and distributing information, and setting international standards for such matters as

A UNICEF water project in Nigeria. Clean water is essential for good health, and ensuring that all people have a pure water supply is a major challenge for the UN.

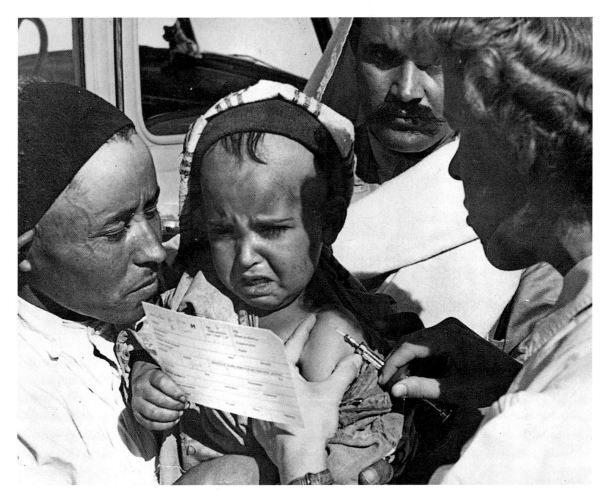

drug purity or water safety. Perhaps the most outstanding example of the WHO's work of coordination was the campaign to eliminate smallpox. In 1980 this disfiguring and often fatal disease was declared to have been eradicated.

A Tunisian child is inoculated against tuberculosis as part of the WHO's campaign to raise the average world-expectation of life to sixty-five years. The WHO's target was to reach thirty million children.

Another part of the WHO's work is aiding individual countries. This can be done through helping to train medical staff, especially doctors, perhaps by providing scholarships. Equipment, such as water filtration plant, can be supplied. Technical information is available, as is money for specific projects.

In the late 1980s the WHO was engaged on an ambitious program to provide "Health for All by the Year 2000." It has concentrated on certain widespread tropical diseases, such as malaria, and on eliminating the six major diseases of children: diphtheria, measles, poliomyelitis, tetanus, tuberculosis and whooping cough. Clean water is another major priority.

No one would deny that the work of the WHO is invaluable, but where do the world's priorities lie? The eradication of smallpox cost $83 million, but although the world spends over $1 trillion annually on arms, a plan to eradicate malaria failed because it could not find the $450 million needed to fund it.

Economic development

Perhaps the most important work of the UN is that of international economic development, yet in no other sphere of its activities, except perhaps that of peacekeeping, are lasting results harder to achieve. In May 1974 the General Assembly solemnly declared its determination to strive for

> . . . *a New International Economic Order, based on equality, sovereignty, interdependence, common interest and cooperation among States, irrespective of their economic and social systems.* [31]

But the problems involved in bringing about a new economic order are as complex as human nature itself.

One of the main difficulties is that most countries in the world have adopted either capitalist or socialist/communist political and economic systems. A capitalist country,

such as the United States, accepts the fact that most human beings are competitive and harnesses that competition to produce more wealth. Some people, therefore, are much better off than others. What happens when this system is applied to international affairs? As countries compete, some become richer and others poorer. In a single country the government can try to do something about differences in wealth through means such as taxation, but this cannot be done internationally.

Socialist or communist states (such as the USSR or China) take a more favorable view of human nature. They believe that people are basically cooperative and that most wealth should be held in common, looked after by the state. If this is to be applied on a global scale, is the UN to take the part played by the government in a single country? The General Assembly's declaration that there ought to be a new economic order irrespective of countries' "economic and social systems" supplies no answer.

International economic and environmental cooperation is vital. Acid rain, the destruction of vast areas of rain forest, and the killing of endangered species of animals are examples of problems for which individual nations could be held responsible but which have an international or global effect. Economic interests often dictate a nation's policy, and it takes powerful (often economic) persuasion to change that policy. International pressure, such as that which the United Nations can apply, can sometimes be effective in this.

The UN seeks to tackle the world's serious economic problems both through its own agencies and by working with affiliated international organizations. The UN's economic program includes: the "'Development Decades" (the 1960s, '70s, and '80s); a Charter of Economic Rights and Duties; international conferences; the UN Development Program (with projects costing over $10 billion); the UN Conference on Trade and Development (to facilitate world trade); the UN Industrial Development Organization; and the UN Environment Program. Economic organizations affiliated with the UN include: the World Bank, the International Development Association, and the International Monetary Fund.

Indian women building a dam. This is the sort of project that UN agencies can help to finance.

Education and other work

"Wars begin in the minds of men, and it is therefore in the minds of men that the defenses of peace must be constructed."[32] These challenging words come from the beginning of the constitution of UNESCO, the United Nations Educational, Scientific and Cultural Organization. In other words, as the constitution continues, UNESCO's task is to promote peace and security by developing education, science and communication.

Yet this aspect of the UN's work, through the agency of UNESCO, is extremely controversial. Much of UNESCO's huge budget ($295,955,000 in 1984) is spent on basic work such as literacy projects, school building and teacher training. The remainder funds international technical programs, cultural matters (the preservation of ancient monuments, for example), and work in the social sciences and communications. It is over these last two that member nations have fallen out. In the 1980s both the United States and Britain left UNESCO.

UNESCO has produced studies on such issues as the tensions leading to war and racism. These have tended to reflect the views of Third World countries, criticizing the West's massive nuclear arsenals, its links with South Africa, and what were seen as provocative military actions, such as the U.S. invasion of Grenada in 1983. The

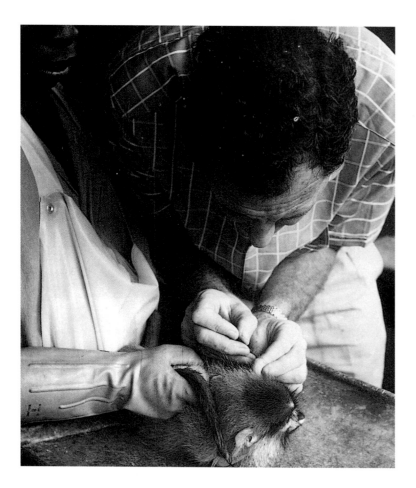

In this WHO training center in Africa an instructor is collecting blood samples from a monkey infected with malaria. The development of scientific education is one of the UN's chief long-term objectives.

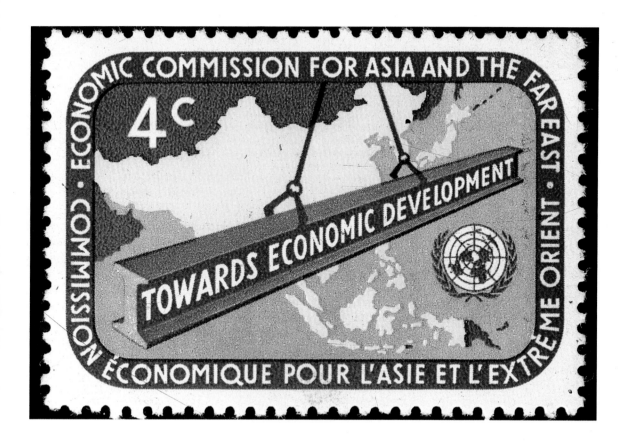

ECONOMIC COMMISSION FOR ASIA AND THE FAR EAST · COMMISSION ÉCONOMIQUE POUR L'ASIE ET L'EXTRÊME ORIENT ·

4c

TOWARDS ECONOMIC DEVELOPMENT

Reagan administration felt that it could no longer continue to subsidize an institution that was regarded as being anti-American in much of its output, and, in 1984, the United States withdrew from UNESCO.

Some commentators have suggested that the motives for the American withdrawal from UNESCO might also be less worthy. In the field of communications UNESCO has an International Program for the Development of Communications, the aim of which is to

> . . . bring about a new information order, through studies of the role of the media in establishing a new economic order, cooperation with regional news agencies, and symposia whose aim is to increase the flow of Third World news.[33]

Much of UNESCO's most important work is often the least spectacular, such as the Universal Postal Union. The UPU standardizes international postal exchanges, aiming to improve postal services and international collaboration. This is one of the UN's stamps.

The trouble is that news can easily carry a political slant. The reporting of racial trouble in South Africa, for example, is very different in that country from the coverage in the United States. American anxiety that Third World news might be made to reflect badly on America's economic strength may have been behind its decision to leave UNESCO. This withdrawal is an example of a nation's willingness to work with others only as long as it feels such cooperation to be immediately beneficial. It may be unrealistic to hope for total and selfless cooperation among governments.

6

THE FUTURE
UN achievements

WHEN THE UNITED NATIONS was being set up in 1945, President Roosevelt cautioned member states against expecting too much from the new organization:

We delude ourselves if we attempt to believe wishfully that all these problems [such as world peace, disarmament, etc.] can be solved overnight . . . Perfectionism, no less than isolationism or imperialism or power politics may obstruct the path to international peace.[34]

It is as well to bear these words in mind when discussing the UN's achievements. If we measure these achievements against the standard of the UN Charter, then they are meager indeed. If, on the other hand, we consider what the UN has done compared with what might have happened if it had

never been called into existence, then its record looks much more positive.

The UN's achievements may be recorded under three headings:

1 Peacekeeping.

Since 1945 there has not been another world war, but that is hardly due to the work of the UN. Small conflicts of terrible ferocity have abounded – from Korea to Afghanistan, from Vietnam to Iran–Iraq. Although the UN has failed to keep the peace, on many occasions it has been the neutral intermediary through which two hostile powers have been able to negotiate. Never was this more important than when Secretary-General U Thant enabled President Kennedy and Premier Khrushchev to make contact with each other during the Cuban missile crisis of 1962. The work of Secretary-General Javier Pérez de Cuéllar in bringing Iran and Iraq together in 1988, after eight years of war, is

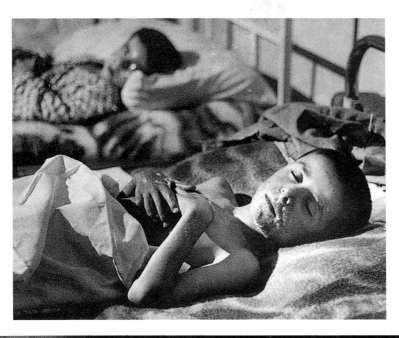

The UN won widespread acclaim for proving the use of chemical weapons in the Iran–Iraq War. Here an Iranian child suffering from chemical burns lies in a hospital visited by UN observers.

◄The Dounreay nuclear power station in Britain. The UN has tried to produce internationally accepted standards for the use of nuclear power, but with limited success.

▼Javier Pérez de Cuéllar, the Peruvian diplomat who became UN Secretary-General in 1982. His untiring international diplomacy has won him world-wide respect.

another example of what the UN has been able to do to bring nations together. The UN cannot keep wars from breaking out, but it can try to bring the warring parties to a negotiating table.

2   Furthering human rights.

The UN has no power to interfere in a country's internal affairs, but it can set standards that are generally agreed upon and draw attention to breaches of these standards, bringing moral pressure to bear on tyrannical governments. Being aware of a problem is surely the first step toward solving it.

3   The provision of aid and the development of international understanding and cooperation.

No one would deny that in this sphere, saving millions from starvation or eliminating disease, the work of the UN and its partner agencies has been outstanding.

Therefore, in some areas the UN has achieved much, while in other fields its record is disappointing. But taking all the aspects of its work together, it does seem that the expensive, cumbersome United Nations Organization has been worthwhile.

The UN's problems

There are many problems and difficulties facing the United Nations. Some of the more important ones are included in the following list.

The domination of the world by superpowers.

Despite the emergence of China, international affairs are still largely dominated by the United States and the USSR. They control massive nuclear arsenals, and struggle with each other to extend their influence to every corner of the globe. The Americans fought in Vietnam to resist communist influence; the Soviets fought in Afghanistan to maintain their hold there. The Security Council cannot operate unless these two are in accord, which has been rare.

The inability of the UN to deal with countries' internal affairs.

A number of crucial issues facing the world today, such as environmental protection, apartheid and terrorism, are largely beyond the scope of the UN. This is particularly worrying in the case of problems, such as pollution, that are international in their effect. Moreover, some nations, particularly the communist ones, tend to be resentful of UN interest in their domestic affairs.

The increase in membership.

Since 1945 the membership of the UN has more than tripled, from 51 to 159. Since each country's vote carries equal weight in the Assembly, the UN can find itself controlled by its numerous but often small Third World members. This frustrates the major powers and has led to a considerable increase in the UN's bureaucracy.

The widening gap between rich and poor nations.

This has increased bitterness and jealousy on the part of the Third World, and suspicion on the part of the wealthier nations.

A TWA hijacking in Beirut. The UN is able to do very little about international terrorism.

The lack of independent finance.

The UN has no more money than its members are prepared to pay. So, when a country feels that its interests are not being served by the UN, it can just reduce its contributions or stop them. For example, this happened with the United States over UNESCO. Substantial sums remain unpaid by the United States (evidence of the hostility of the Reagan administration to the UN) and, to a lesser extent, by the USSR, threatening the UN with bankruptcy.

Despite all its efforts, famine remains a major international problem for the UN. Only the most far-sighted national politicians accept the mutual interdependence of all the countries of the world.

The failure of the Security Council to provide independent UN forces.

Except in the case of Korea, the UN has never been able to agree to assemble a major independent force. The UN's role as a peacekeeper has thus been limited.

Nationalism and internationalism will always conflict.

There is a conflict when a government is faced with a decision that will harm itself, but be to the benefit of the international community. For example, Brazil is reluctant to harm its country's economy by ceasing to exploit the Amazon rain forest, even though such development is believed to be upsetting the ecology of the whole world.

Reform of the UN

Several changes in the way the UN is organized have been suggested. The first is in the field of finance. Although the UN has a massive budget, which it generally spends wisely and carefully, the amount of money it receives is tiny compared with its needs, and compared with the budgets of the member nations. Britain's contribution, for example, amounts to about one percent of its defense budget. Perhaps it would be wiser for a country's contribution to be a fixed percentage of its Gross National Product, collected automatically. There might be some way of preventing a member state from withholding funds because it disagrees with a particular project.

The Secretariat of the UN might be improved by giving the Secretary-General and his staff a more positive role in the world, and by coordinating the many diverse programs in which the UN is involved. At present, it is very difficult to keep track of the thousands of different projects, some of which overlap, and some of which are not really necessary.

The UN's Headquarters in New York. The low building with a concave wedged roof-line houses the General Assembly. Some people think that the UN should be based in a neutral country, such as Switzerland.

Kampuchean refugees living on the Thai border. Kampuchea's seat in the UN is held by a three-party coalition that includes the Khmer Rouge – the brutal party responsible for the deaths of well over one million Kampucheans.

It has been realized that, with a vote for each member state, the Assembly is dominated by poor countries from the Third World with not many inhabitants. Perhaps very poor or small countries should become associate members, with the right to speak but not the right to vote on important issues. In the case of the Security Council, many people argue that its ten elected members should be more representative of the major world powers. There could also be more private meetings, where members do not have to present an image to the world looking on.

Apart from structural reforms, a change in emphasis for the UN has been recommended. It must accept that it cannot prevent wars, or even solve disputes, and concentrate on what it can do best, for example, its work in the social, economic and technological fields. On the issue of disputes, the words of Sir Anthony Parsons, Britain's representative at the UN from 1979 to 1982, are a useful guide:

Problems are only solved peacefully between the parties themselves: the function of the UN is at most to draw up broad guidelines, to use its mediating mechanism to bring parties together and its peacekeeping capabilities to confirm ceasefires and truces, and thus create the atmosphere in which negotiations can proceed.[35]

Toward a united world

In 1959, when the major powers were locked in a cold war that seemed to threaten nuclear holocaust, the Soviet leader Nikita Khrushchev wrote these words:

Part of a mural from inside the UN Conference Building in New York. The theme of the huge mural is mankind's struggle for a lasting peace. It begins with the destruction of a family and ends with its resurrection, looking toward a generation of peace.

> *By the scale of modern technology our planet is not very big . . . You may like your neighbor or dislike him. You are not obliged to be friends with him or visit him. But you live side by side, and what can you do if neither you nor he has any desire to quit the old home and move to another town? All the more so in relations between states. It would be unreasonable to assume that you can make it so hot for your undesirable neighbor that he will decide to move to Mars or Venus. And vice versa, of course.*
>
> *What else can be done? There may be two ways out: either war . . . or peaceful coexistence. Whether you like your neighbor or not, nothing can be done about it, you have to find some way of getting on with him, for we live on one planet.*[36]

This is why the UN, for all its faults, mistakes and imperfections, must survive. Not only must it survive, but it must be strengthened.

The world is faced with great problems: nuclear confrontation could destroy the planet in minutes; pollution could kill it slowly over the coming decades. The end result of either tragedy is the same. There are no solutions yet to the problems of the growing world population, the sweeping famines that devastate whole nations, the widening gulf between rich and poor countries, or the need to find safe, practical energy resources that will last well into the future.

Only international cooperation can solve these problems, and the only international organization with the potential for arranging such cooperation is the United Nations. Many people are scornful of the UN because of its weaknesses, but they have nothing to put in its place. Its headquarters is criticized for being just a talking club; but to provide opportunities for people of different nations to talk to each other is surely an achievement in itself.

After more than ten years as Secretary-General of the UN, Kurt Waldheim wrote the following words, which provide a fitting and positive comment on the future of the United Nations:

I do not expect miracles or spectacular successes. Sound political progress is seldom based on either. But I am convinced that the United Nations provides the best road to the future for those who have confidence in our capacity to shape our own fate on this planet.[37]

The German nuclear power station at Bibis where there was a serious accident in December 1987. Incidents such as this, and the nuclear disaster at Chernobyl in 1986, bring home to people of every nation, race and creed the fact that they all share the same vulnerable planet.

Important dates

Date	Events
1919	Foundation of the League of Nations
1931	Japanese invasion of Manchuria
1933	Hitler comes to power
1938–39	Hitler seizes Czechoslovakia
1939	Outbreak of World War II, collapse of the League of Nations
1941	Atlantic Charter
1945	International Monetary Fund established
	Principles for a UN agreed by Churchill, Roosevelt and Stalin at Yalta Conference
	End of World War II
	United Nations established in San Francisco and *(October 24)* the General Assembly first meets in London
1946	United Nations Educational, Scientific and Cultural Organization (UNESCO) founded
	Court of International Justice reestablished
1947	UN mediates in Palestine
1948	World Health Organization (WHO) established
	General Agreement on Tariffs and Trade (GATT) comes into force
	UN mediates in Kashmir and in Arab–Israeli conflict
	Universal Declaration of Human Rights adopted by UN
1949	Communists come to power in China
	NATO formed
1950	USSR boycotts Security Council
	UN peace force actively involved in Korea (to 1953)
	United Nations Children's Fund (UNICEF) established
	UN High Commissioner for Refugees appointed
1953	Death of Stalin; Malenkov becomes Premier of USSR
1955	Warsaw Pact formed
1956	USSR invades Hungary
	Suez crisis: UN organizes ceasefire in Middle East and provides a peacekeeping force
	International Atomic Energy Authority established
1957	European Economic Community (EEC) formed
1959	Treaty banning nuclear weapons from Antarctic arranged by UN
1960	Congolese civil war (to 1964) – UN successfully involved
1961	J. F. Kennedy elected president of United States
1962	UN mediates in Indonesia
	Cuban missile crisis: UN Secretary-General mediates between United States and USSR
1963	President Kennedy assassinated
1964	UN mediates in Cyprus
	China detonates atomic bomb
	United Nations Conference on Trade and Development (UNCTAD) established
1965	United States openly enters war in Vietnam
	Security Council membership increased from 11 to 15
	UNICEF awarded Nobel Peace Prize
	Ceasefire in Kashmir arranged by UN
1966	Treaty banning nuclear weapons from outer space arranged by UN
1967	Six-Day War: UN organizes ceasefire between Israel and Arabs
	General Assembly accepts the Declaration on the Elimination of Discrimination against Women

Date	Events
1968	USSR invades Czechoslovakia
	Nuclear non-proliferation treaty
	Richard Nixon elected president of United States
1969	United Nations Fund for Population Activities established
1970	Treaty banning nuclear weapons from ocean bed organized by UN
1971	UN Fund for Drug Abuse Control set up
	Communist China enters UN
1972	UN supervises "line of control" between India and Pakistan
	UN convention against bacteriological warfare
	President Nixon visits China and the USSR
	UN Conference on the Human Environment, Stockholm
	SALT 1 Treaty
1973	Yom Kippur war: UN ceasefire between Israel and Arabs
	U.S. troops leave Vietnam
1974	Turkish forces invade Cyprus: UN forces swept aside
	UN establishes its Special Committee Against Apartheid, and World Food Council
1976	Soweto riots in South Africa
1978	Special UN session on disarmament
1979	USSR invades Afghanistan
	United States arranges settlement between Israel and Egypt at Camp David
	SALT 2 Treaty
1980	Smallpox declared eradicated
	Iran–Iraq War breaks out
	Ronald Reagan elected president of United States
1982	Israeli invasion of Lebanon
	Falklands/Malvinas War
1983	UN convention on ocean bed prepared
	United States invades Grenada
1984	Geneva Arms Talks between United States and USSR
1986	Chernobyl nuclear accident
	State of Emergency declared in South Africa
1987	Intermediate Range Missile Treaty between United States and USSR
1988	Pérez de Cuéllar acts to bring Iran and Iraq to negotiations
	UN reveals, and condemns, use of chemical weapons in Iran–Iraq conflict

Glossary

Agency	An organization that undertakes work on behalf of another.
Apartheid	The South African policy of "separate development" for white and black people.
Arbitrate	To attempt to achieve a settlement between parties.
Boycott	To refuse to deal with an organization or nation.
Budget	The amount of money that is available, and the plan for its expenditure
Bureaucracy	A system of administration organized into strict divisions of departments and bureaus run by officials.
Capitalism	An economic theory that believes in the virtue of free enterprise and the right to individual property and wealth.
Cold War	A term for the hostile and suspicious relations between East and West that began after World War II but never actually resulted in fighting
Colony	Overseas territory administered and ruled by another country.
Commission	A group that is instructed to carry out a particular task.
Communism	A political and economic theory based on the ideas of Karl Marx who believed in the abolition of private property and the creation of a classless society.
Conventional weapons	Non-nuclear weapons.
Covenant	A binding agreement.
Discrimination	Unfair favoring of one side or group of people, often because of a characteristic such as race, color, sex or religion.
Dissidents	Those who disagree with the official government or party line.
Ethics	A set of moral values or principles.
Gross National Product	The total value of all the goods and services produced annually by a nation.
Human rights	Certain rights all people should be allowed, for example, liberty, justice, freedom from torture and no imprisonment without trial.
Ideology	The beliefs or set of principles of a nation or political system.
Imperialism	Policy of making or maintaining an empire by taking over other states.
Impotence	Lacking power.
INF	Intermediate Nuclear Force – weapons with a range of 500–5,000 kilometers (310–3,100 mi).
Integrity	Moral honesty.
Intermediary	A person who acts as a go-between to parties in a dispute.
Internationalism	The practice of cooperation and understanding between different nations.
Islam	The Muslim religion.
Isolationism	The policy of avoiding, as far as possible, contact with other states.
Mandate	A former colony or other occupied territory that was looked after by another country under League of Nations supervision.
Mediate	To act as an intermediary (*q.v.*).
Nationalism	Patriotism, or the desire to put the interests of one's nation before the wider interests of other nations and the world.
Negotiate	Attempt to solve a problem by discussion.

Plebiscite	A vote taken by the electorate of a state on a question of national importance.
Protagonist	One of the participants in a quarrel.
Ratify	To approve officially.
Refugee	A person who has fled his or her country because of some danger or propblem, such as war or political persecution.
Resolution	A formal agreement or judgement, which may condemn an event or recommend action but holds no power to enforce the decision.
SALT	Strategic Arms Limitation Talks.
Sanctions	Refusing to trade or have official dealings with a nation, as a way of forcing that nation to agree to a decision or alter its policy on something.
Socialism	An economic theory that believes that the state should own all important means of production and distribution of wealth.
Stockpile	To acquire a large quantity of something and store it until it is required.
Strategy	A plan of campaign – for war, business, or politics.
Superpower	One of the world's major military powers.
Terrorism	Use of violence or intimidation (for example bombing, kidnapping) to force a government to agree to demands.
Treaty	An agreement between two or more nations concerning their future relationship.
Tyranny	A rule or authority that is oppressive and unjust.
Veto	To prevent legislation or action proposed by others by voting against it.

Further reading

Carroll, Raymond, *The Future of the United Nations*. Franklin Watts, 1985*
Chomsky, Noam, *Towards a New Cold War*. Pantheon, 1982
Harrison. S. M., *World Conflict in the Twentieth Century*. Macmillan, 1987*
Koral, April, *An Album of War Refugees*. Franklin Watts, 1989*
La Feber, Walter, *America, Russia, and the Cold War, 1945–1984*. Wiley, 1985
Laqueur, Walter, *Europe Since Hitler*. Penguin, 1982
Laqueur, Walter and Rubin, Barry M., *The Israel–Arab Reader*. Penguin, 1984
Palmer, Alan, *Facts on File Dictionary of Twentieth Century History*. Facts on File
Palmer, Alan, *The Penguin Dictionary of Twentieth Century History 1789–1945*. Penguin, 1984*
Stavrianos, L. S., *Global Rift: The Third World Comes of Age*. Prentice Hall, 1981
Woods, Harold & Geraldine, *The United Nations*. Franklin Watts, 1985*
Vadney, T. E., *The World Since 1945*. Penguin, 1987*

* Easier books

Notes on sources

1 *New English Bible,* Isaiah II, 4.
2 Cited in Richard Hofstadter (ed.), *Great Issues in American History from Reconstruction to the Present Day 1864–1969,* Vintage Books, 1969, p. 226.
3 *Ibid.,* p. 237.
4 Cited in S. R. Gibbons and P. Morican, *The League of Nations and the UNO,* Longman, 1970, p. 64.
5 Hofstadter, *op. cit.,* pp. 407–9.
6 The Charter of the United Nations is widely available.
7 *Basic Facts about the United Nations,* UN, 1985, p. 1.2.
8 Kurt Waldheim, *The Challenge of Peace,* Weidenfeld and Nicolson, 1980, p. 2.
9 Evan Luard, *The United Nations,* Macmillan, 1979, p. 54.
10 Kurt Waldheim, *op. cit.,* p. 1.
11 Evan Luard, *op. cit.,* p. 101.
12 *Basic Facts about the United Nations,* p. 1.11.
13 Kurt Waldheim, *In the Eye of the Storm,* Weidenfeld and Nicolson, 1985, p. 265.
14 *United Nations Image and Reality,* UN, 1986, p. 18.
15 *Basic Facts about the United Nations,* p. 11.12.
16 Brian Urquhart, *Hammarskjöld,* Bodley Head, 1972, p. 7.
17 Cited in W. Laqueur and B. Rubin, *The Israel-Arab Reader,* Penguin, 1984, p. 125.
18 *Ibid.,* p. 676.
19 *Ibid.,* p. 224.
20 Richard Nixon, *Memoirs,* Grosset and Dunlap, 1978, pp. 824, 922.
21 Kurt Waldheim, *In the Eye of the Storm,* p. 78.
22 G. R. Berridge, *International Politics,* Wheatsheaf Books, 1987, pp. 188–9.
23 Cited in Brian Urquhart, *op. cit.,* p. 398.
24 *Ibid.,* p. 459.
25 Evan Luard, *A History of the United Nations,* Vol. 1, Macmillan, 1982, p. 341.
26 Pérez de Cuéllar, cited in Victoria Schofield, *The United Nations,* Wayland, 1979, p. 39.
27 Kurt Waldheim, *The Challenge of Peace,* p. 45.
28 Cited in S. M. Harrison, *World Conflict in the Twentieth Century,* Macmillan, 1987, p. 350.
29 Article 55 of the UN Charter.
30 *Basic Facts about the United Nations,* p. VII.6.
31 *Ibid.,* p. 111.2.
32 Cited in Jacob A. Rubin, *Pictorial History of the United Nations,* Thomas Yaseloff, 1962, p. 217.
33 *Basic Facts about the United Nations,* p. VII.6.
34 Cited in Rubin, *op. cit.,* p. 82.
35 From an article in the *Independent,* July 26, 1988.
36 *On Peaceful Coexistence,* Moscow, 1961, pp. 77–8.
37 Kurt Waldheim, *The Challenge of Peace,* p. 119.

Picture acknowledgments

The author and publisher would like to thank the following for allowing their illustrations to be reproduced in this book: Mary Evans 4, 5 (top and bottom), 6, 7; Hutchison 42; John Jensen and *Sunday Telegraph* 16; David Low and *Evening Standard* 8, 44; David Low and *Daily Herald* 14; Photri 54; Popperfoto 9 (top and bottom), 12, 15 (bottom), 19, 23, 27, 28, 33, 36, 38, 39, 41, 48, 49 (top); Strube and *Daily Express* 34; Topham 10, 11 (bottom), 15 (top), 17 (top and bottom), 18, 21, 29, 31 (top and bottom), 32, 35 (top and bottom), 37, 40, 43, 45, 46, 49 (bottom), 50, 51, 53, 55; United Nations 20; Zec and *Daily Mirror* 11 (top). Thanks also to the Centre for the Study of Cartoons and Caricature, University of Kent at Canterbury. The maps were supplied by Thames Cartographic Services Ltd., and the diagram on page 13 by Malcolm Walker.

Index